*To Nan
My Kindred
Sister
♡ Rebecca*

REBECCA GILBERT, BEd., MEd.

THE PRINCIPALS' HANDBOOK

A RESOURCE FOR PROFESSIONAL LEADERSHIP IN EDUCATION

The Principals' Handbook
Copyright © 2017 by Rebecca Gilbert, BEd., MEd.

No part of this publication may be reproduced, distributed, or transmitted in any form or by any means, including photocopying, recording, or other electronic or mechanical methods, without the prior written permission of the author, except in the case of brief quotations embodied in critical reviews and certain other non-commercial uses permitted by copyright law.

tellwell

Tellwell Talent
www.tellwell.ca

ISBN
978-1-77302-617-6 (Paperback)

A Resource
For
Professional Leadership
In Education

Dedication

This handbook is dedicated
to the principals of the Catholic Independent Schools of the Diocese of Prince George (CISPG). Without you, this handbook would not have been possible. Your words of wisdom, educational leadership and collaborative sharing over many meetings, gatherings and dialogues flow throughout these pages.

Deep gratitude goes to my 'chosen school family' of Sacred Heart School.
To our "Panther-land" where we have learned, grown and celebrated together all the blessings of our 'day-to-day' journey these past years.

To my sons, Finbar and Aedan. Without you, my life would not be complete.
I treasure the gift of Motherhood.

To the Giver of All Life, to whom I have served and dedicated my life.
To You all praise and gratitude is given.

Contents

Forward: Collective Wisdom

A word before we begin...

Abstract

1. "The Passing of the Guard" - **Keys**
2. "There's NO Posse Behind You" - **Jump In**
3. "It's How We Roll" - **School Culture**
4. "Focus on the Little People" - **Stay Student Focused**
5. "Know Who You are Agent for" - **Policy, Procedures, Protocol**
6. "Polite, Positive and Professional" - **Communication**
7. "Keep Your Own Counsel" - **Privacy**
8. "Leave a Trail" - **Document!**
9. "It's NOT in the Manual" - **Trust Yourself**
10. "The Acorn doesn't Fall Far from the Tree" - **Parents**
11. "Who's Free for Breakfast?" - **Collective Wisdom**
12. "Hiring, Mentoring and Resignations" – **Educational Leadership**
13. "Thank Them, Feed Them, Celebrate Them" - **Staff**
14. "Standing on the Shoulders of Giants" - **The Role of the Elders**
15. "Let's Celebrate this Moment" - **Giving Thanks**
16. "Let Us Pray" -**Faith-based Schools**
17. "Tapping Out" - **What You Leave Behind.**

Keep Moving Forward

After Thoughts

Acknowledgements

- o Leadership and Professional Resource List

FORWARD: Collective Wisdom... This book is not at all what I expected it would be when Rebecca Gilbert first said she was going to undertake the task of writing something for principals. Over many meetings and phone calls in the first years of her principalship, when faced with the challenges of being a new principal, she often expressed her frustration, "Why don't we have a handbook? This should be written down somewhere!" So, when I settled down to read this principals' handbook, I expected to read something that was prescriptive, perhaps a detailed list of 'how to's' that a principal could pick up and refer to in times of crisis.

That is not what you will get here. It goes far deeper than that!

This book will challenge you to the very core! It will demand that you invest the time to reflect on why you have taken on this role of being a principal. It will challenge you to know what is really important in the huge enterprise of running a school, a place of learning, where children need to be at the heart of everything you do. It will help you to understand that you need bucket loads of passion, persistence and gratitude. It will soothe you in knowing that you will not always get it right, in fact some days will seem like you can't get *anything* right. It will insist on a growth mindset based on reflective practice as a way to become the best that you can be.

At the end of the day, this handbook will help you get your priorities right. It will convince you that you need to be in this business for the sake of the children, for the sake of the learners and for service. Rebecca's passion will inspire you to think deeply, tap into your inner strengths, and stride forward boldly. Great principals are passionate about their school, their community and most of all their students. They are visionaries, lighting the way along the path to success. May the collective wisdom in this handbook light the way for you to step easier, more assuredly as a guide to help find your way as principal.

Donncha O'Callaghan,
Principal of Immaculate Conception School

A word before we begin…

Leading a group of people can be a daunting task. Leading a school community can be even more daunting, especially if you are in a new role as the principal. The purpose of this handbook is to act as a guide to you on this journey. The collective wisdom is distilled with many thought-provoking statements; from the practical to the profound. Even the most experienced principal may find something to 'ponder, chew and digest'. While not every practical point will be covered, what is brought forward will "stretch" you as a professional – causing you to ask more questions, digging deeper and uncovering your own growing edges. The focus of this handbook is to provide you with sufficient communal wisdom to use as a 'stepping stone' to propel you forward. It is my hope that it will relieve some of the pressure that comes with this wonderful, intimidating and inspiring profession.

Looking ahead, go easy on yourself. Your role as a principal is important and purposeful work. Hold fast and steady, and be willing to be moulded by your staff, students and unpredictable events where no two days are alike. One of the most honest and helpful statements principals with years of experience have shared with me is: *'Student focused work is what's important. The rest won't matter in the end'.*
The journey is long, full of twists and turns, but you are not alone. Trust in knowing that you are where you are for a reason, and even if you do not know what that is yet, it will be revealed. Trust the process.

Blessings on your journey!

Rebecca

Abstract of Terms:

Principal: The individual in charge of the educational, managerial and, if applicable, spiritual leadership in the school. This differs from the term Administrator. Principals are 'people' focused. It is people who are important to a Principal.

Mentor Teacher: An experienced teacher that leads staff in particular areas of development and growth. Mentor teachers have the character, knowledge and experience that other professionals in the building may not.

Novice Teacher: A new teacher who does not have the experience or knowledge of the school culture, curriculum, or experiential wisdom that the mentor teacher encapsulates.

School Culture: The very essence and vibe of the school's hospitality, structure and purpose. School culture is the energy you see and feel as soon as you walk through the doors, and that pours forth beyond the doors into the greater community.

Educator: Those who use their education, expertise, life skills or experience to teach, guide and nurture students and colleagues alike.

Affirmation: A positive or constructive comment or statement that contributes to the growth of individuals.

Journey: The day-to-day moving forward that is both individual and collective; a way of being together.

"The Passing of the Guard" Keys

"Do not rush a decision in a stressful or troubling situation. Listen, seek advice, and contemplate before arriving at a conclusion. New beginnings can be difficult."
Tamara Berg

Sitting in the "Principal's Chair" can mean many things to different people. Some look at it as a place of power, either earned or unearned. Some take the role of principal as a position of prestige or status, and perhaps the role is seen that way from the outside. I can assure you, however, no matter how you view your new position, if lived well, it is a "seat of service." Although, believe me, sitting is something you will rarely be doing!

The morning I received the 'keys to the castle' was one of the most nerve-wracking moments in my life. It was also one of the loneliest, anxious days of my professional journey. Once the information the previous principal deemed vital was exchanged and the keys were in hand, I looked around my new surroundings. It was August 1st and the building that had held and housed generations of students, staff and educators on a yearly basis now stood in deafening silence. As I walked through the empty ancient halls, with the smell of its history filling my nostrils, I knew my life would be forever changed. This was not just a new job I was about to begin. This was a new chapter in my life, a new vocation, a new kind of 'YES' on the journey that I did not feel fully prepared for, although others saw the potential that was there. As I climbed stairs, explored rooms, and walked corridors, a phrase I often heard my mother share came to mind. "Leave it better than you found it." Looking down at the 11 keys that were now in my possession, I had no idea which keys opened which doors. In those very first moments, my hopeful, terrified heart knew I had to leave the school in a better state than I had found it.

Although I had been assured of a team that would help me at any turn, I also realized there would now be a 'deliberate loneliness' that was also a given when taking on the role of principal. Deliberate loneliness is knowing there would be times when I would be alone in making certain decision. It was not a gift I necessarily wanted or desired. I also knew I would take the flack for decisions that were not always mine, and I would choose silence knowing the bigger picture transpiring around certain decisions were not mine to share. I would have to step into the unknown, do the unthinkable, and get to know the team and staff who would be watching my every move. However, no matter how fearful it all seemed in the moment, my mother's voice encouraged me forward to 'leave the school, staff, and students better than I had found them'. I needed to trust the motherly wisdom that all things indeed were possible.

> "There would now be a 'deliberate loneliness' that was a given when taking on the role of principal. A gift I did not necessarily want or desire".

Points to Ponder:

1. Why did you take on this profession at this stage of your life?
2. How will you leave your school/staff better than you found them? What gifts do you bring? What gifts will you call forth from others?
3. Recall your introduction to this new position. What would you do differently when it is time for you to pass on the 'keys to the castle' to the next principal? What were you grateful for from that past experience that you will take into the present?'
4. When was a time that you faced 'deliberate loneliness' and what was that experience for you? What interior resources do you draw upon in making a decision alone?

Action Items:

- Walk around your school with 'fresh eyes' and see what needs to be made a little better than how you found it. Fresh eyes can be a gift to a school.
- Make a list of items that can be done in a week, month, year or as a long term project.
- Notice what you find appealing and exciting in your school. What already exists that can be expanded on that may enrich the school culture?

Reflections:_____
_____
_____
_____
_____
_____
_____
_____
_____
_____
_____
_____
_____
_____
_____
_____
_____
_____

"There's NO Posse Behind You" Jump In

"It was told to me that the most important degree you need for principalship is a degree in common sense and I've found this to be true. Thinking on your feet, staying calm, being able to laugh at yourself, and taking time to reflect are all key parts of the principal's day." Donncha O'Callaghan

At the beginning of any new task there is always a sense of fear of the unknown. Fear is a part of leadership that one needs to learn to embrace. Standard 'pious platitudes' posted at eye level such as 'FEAR: False Evidence Appearing Real" or 'What doesn't kill you makes you stronger' can be helpful. Mantras and sticky notes with positive affirmations may also be helpful. I have come to understand that the best way to face fear is to 'befriend' it. Face forward and lean into it. Principals need to be courageous and brave, and often this does not come easily. Fear may lessen at different times in our life, and its power over us can become weaker. However, fear can also stay in the shadows and rear its head at unexpected moments. It is usually in the lonely, hungry, tired moments of our week that it comes knocking. Fear is a 'built in' part of our human nature that comes from a primal instinct for survival. Fear is also a learned behaviour that comes from past experiences that colour the way we see a current event or encounter. In sharing stories with principals who have journeyed two to thirty-two years in this profession, they acknowledge their sleepless nights, obsessive replaying of situations, moments of doubt, and sudden decision-making that fill them with anxiety. Second-guessing a decision you make is part-and-parcel of your first year to your twentieth year and beyond.

What I have found helpful when fear 'befriends' me during a day of decision-making or as a stealer of night time rest is to look squarely at the situation and celebrate even the smallest victory that has helped move the situation forward. Whether it is that phone call made with the difficult parent, or that series of emails giving a sensitive response, or even the first presentation made to teachers on a difficult topic. Give thanks for the small successes. Fearful moments will show up. Lean forward and befriend them. They are only as big as you make them. Face the fear squarely head on. Keep stepping forward, cautiously perhaps, but forward. Fearful moments will show up but you control how long they get to stay. Do not entertain them long. Create a support system that can be a sounding board for you and place trusted people in your school strategically so assistance is on site when situations become fearful. Choose your key people carefully. They will be your support system and be clear about expectations around confidentiality and trust.

One KEY main support when starting your principalship:

Choose your *Teacher In Charge* wisely. See who had the role before you and discern this position well. You want a trusted colleague who will celebrate with you and support you even when you make mistakes. This person may become a deeply trusted ally.

Make a **Teacher In Charge** (TIC) binder.

1. Have the following ten top things for a TIC:
    1) Principals' contact info where you will be : phone, email etc.
    2) Where you will be: Hotel, conference etc.
    3) Contact information for all staff
    4) Crisis Situation Protocol List: include Liaison Officer and School Counsellor, Superintendent etc.
    5) Sub list for teachers/Educational Assistants
    6) Parent contact sheets and student list
    7) Safety procedures
    8) Superintendent phone number and information
    9) Contact information for principals' you trust and are close by in case of emergency.

10) 'Check in' accountability record for all teachers

2. Who is the teacher in charge? What are her/his strengths and weakness? Choose the *second* in command that compliments the TIC. Make sure one of them knows the students well and has the trust of the staff.

3. Talk to other principals about what their expectations are for their Teacher In Charge. Touch base by phone or email with your TIC everyday if possible when absent. This shows support and gives an opportunity for you to THANK them for what they do in your absence.

> "When fear 'befriends' me during a day of decision-making or as a stealer of night-time rest is to look squarely at the situation and celebrate even the smallest victory that has helped move the situation forward."

Points to Ponder:
1. What is it you are most afraid of in your principal's role?
2. How can you respond creatively when fear rears its head and starts to become a constant companion the first year?
3. Who are the trusted colleagues you will share fearful moments with as you lean forward in this role?

Action Items:
- Make a list of the ways you will befriend fear.
- Call or email the trusted companions and share a fear that you are experiencing about your position. Listen to a situation that makes them fearful.
- Observe staff and students as they move about their day in your school community. Know they too share similar and different fears as a part of our human nature.

Reflections:

"It's How We Roll" School Culture

"School culture is the most important, most difficult, never ending responsibility of an educational and school leader. The culture or climate is born of respect and dignity, and a genuine love of children, by all the adults in your community." Dave Crawley

School culture is the very essence and vibe of your building. It has the *'who, what, where and how long'* that walk the halls every day. The dress code, the bulletin boards, and the buzz on the playground all contribute to the energy of your school. It is this spirit that fills the air. It encompasses the attitude of your students' pride and the staff's demeanour as well as your school council's attitude and parents' outlook that all become the threads to the fabric that make up your school community. Remember, you as the principal set the tone. You will rely on crucial people such as the person in your front office who monitors the coming and goings. The person who greets everyone that comes through the front door, your maintenance person whom you call at all hours, and your custodian who cleans up all that you leave behind each day. Mesh these personalities together with the eclectic dispositions of your staff members, the backgrounds of your students, the wider community, and the history of your educational building. All these woven together make for an interesting, vital starting point.

Your efforts will enrich what is present, build on the greatness gone before you, or in some cases try to nurse back to health the unhealthy, toxic school community that is crumbling. No matter what you inherited, school culture matters. It can be built. It can be changed and it must be celebrated for the longevity of your school community. The most important part of school culture is that it must be student focused. Parents, educators, staff, and community professionals, will buy into school culture because what unites is stronger than what divides. Personality conflicts, differing perspectives, even financial struggles can be worked through when school culture is strong. Let it always be about the students. Listen, learn, and understand the school culture when you take on the leadership role of your particular enterprise. The smells, the sounds, and the energy of the building are what permeate the spirit you will work in every day. This will also indicate what kind of learning, education and experiences the future will hold for all who walk its halls. If the school culture is weak or not positive, this is an action item requiring immediate attention. Be purposeful in trying to change it!

School culture will determine growth patterns, how long your teachers stay and how open your parents feel about becoming involved in school events. Parent participation is vital within your school community. Positivity breeds positivity, negativity breeds negativity. This basic karmic value is not to be minimized. We know there will be moments when tensions will arise in the building. Such as when staff are tired or students are close to major holidays like Christmas, Spring, or Summer Break. The whole energy may shift within your building at these times. They are anticipated energy changers that hard work and good learning flow into. During these energy shifts, large doses of patience, humour and good cheer will be needed. Celebrate a tired staff with affirmation and re-affirmation. Celebrate restless, eager students with focused activities, physical pursuits, and busyness. Celebrate holiday 'break times' with freedom, surrender, and a gentle resting space for everyone that is part of the learning community, including yourself.

Listen long and carefully to the mentor teachers. These professionals have been around to see more than one set of students graduate from the doors of your building. Questions to ask yourself as you are learning the school culture that currently exists are: "What parents are standing in your playground in the morning?" "What socio-economic average of vehicles do you have coming and going in your parking lot?" "Who is dropping off students and who is walking from within the neighbourhood?" "What kinds of families are attracted to your school?" "What is the niche your school offers to the community?" "What are the community's triumphs and legacies that are being retold?" "What are the memories they are trying to forget and leave behind?" Be attentive and keep your eyes and ears open to the various comings and goings of parents and students. Lastly, and perhaps something not given enough credence, however, is your starting point: talk to the students. It is ALL about the students.

In the morning get out and greet students by their names. Become familiar with siblings and family members. Be aware of the weekend happenings and what are the anticipated Friday evening activities for your students. At times, it can be difficult to do this as the paperwork, communications, and deadlines tend to pile up for a principal. Remember: people before paper. This is the key component to your role. Keeping a pulse on your school community starts with what is happening on the playground. Be present where parents, students and teachers mingle before school in the morning, during recesses, and at the end of the students' day. The playground is often the place where you can 'hype' up victory or 'put out the fires' before difficulties start to flame and enter the hallways of learning. Simple observations and conversations let people know you are present, available, and part of the community. It is a visible sign you are willing to take time to greet and share in the stories of their personal lives. It lets people know that what is important to them is also important to you; what is heart breaking for them is also heartbreaking for you. Be present. Meet people face to face. Early on you will notice all are carrying heavy burdens. Be willing to help those who share the path coming to and from your school.

Understanding your school culture will reveal many things of which you may want to take note. If you are in an inner city or often called Tier-One school, the culture will be vastly different from a Tier-Three school. Worrying about drug needles, people in stairwells, or questionable litter on your playground each morning is a very different challenge than worrying about hovering helicopter parents questioning your every move. The most important thing to remember is to keep student focused. A good question to ask yourself as a check in, "Would I want my own son or daughter growing and learning in this school environment?" If the answer is no, change it. If it is yes, build on it and celebrate it.

> "School Culture will determine your growth patterns, how long your teachers will stay, and how open your parents will feel to become involved in your school community."

Points to Ponder:
1. How would you describe your school's culture?
2. Is the energy one of hope, learning and possibilities? Is there a positive spirit that you look forward to encountering everyday? Or is the energy toxic and needing to change? What needs to be enhanced and what needs to be corrected?
3. What are the demographics of the families that are your school community? How does this affect your school?

Action Items:
- Try to be the first on the playground for a month and greet all the students and staff by name each morning.
- Ask the students on Friday lunch what their plans are for the weekend. Note to self what you learn from the sharing.
- Understand that your bird's eye view of the students' life on the playground is magnified in the classroom. Support your teachers in what they need for optimal learning to take place.

Reflections:_____
_____
_____

"Focus on the Little People" Stay Student Focused

"The students are my boss. I work for them. Without them, this would be an empty building." Terri Haynal

Students are the same wherever you go. Personalities, personal needs, cultures may differ and the vulnerability index of families may shift and change. However, at the root, students are students and need support, care, and positive modelling by adults. Students need positive people in their corner to believe in them and encourage them. Students also need that soft place to fall when life is overwhelming and they are not receiving that support needed for optimum growth. As educators, we are that due diligent parent. I believe in the age-old wisdom of "it take a village to raise a child." Staying student focused will not lead you astray. Provide the best you can for students' needs to be met.

Here are ten areas to note when working with students:

1. Safety is always your first and utmost concern: Keeping the students safe and having safety protocols and procedures in place is the main priority in any school. Make sure these are in place before anything else. Do not bend on safety policies, protocol or procedures. There may be times staff will want to overlook these. Remind them the safety of the children is your first priority. Your defining line in the sand is first and foremost: safety for all people in your building.

2. Do what is best for students: When implementing programs (e.g. deciding where to spend the budget monies or which speakers to bring into your building) ask yourself the question "Is this in the best interest of my students?" This is true for whether it is the lyrics of a song for assembly, what literature you bring into your school library and classrooms to what the new logo will look like in your gym. Always keep the interests of your students in the forefront.

3. Do what is best for your most vulnerable learners: Schools have a variety of students with different needs. Once students cross the threshold of your doors, their different learning needs become your responsibility. When creating a rule, protocol, or an event, ponder what it will mean for your most vulnerable learners. There will be students who require extra care and attention and ones whose presence will grace your office as a principal more than others. Connect with them inside and outside your office. Build relationships with them, find out what is important to them and make them a priority. If vulnerable learners are succeeding, everyone will be succeeding. The most vulnerable learners are your barometer for a variety of levels of success, whether social-emotional, academics, sporting events or the arts. All need to be included for your school to succeed.

4. Meet basic needs: Maslow's hierarchy of needs indicates that the basic needs of food, water, and sleep must first to be met before any learning and growth can happen. This is an important point to remember when dealing with students. If a child is in your office before 10 am, find out if they have had breakfast, how much sleep they have had, and what was their morning routine. Students in your office at this time usually have basic needs that have not yet been met. Provide for them what they need so they can learn.

5. Life skills: There is a greater need in society today to teach life skills than ever before. Manners, etiquette, general respect for others, care for the elderly, care for the environment as well as simple kindness seem to be a challenge for many young people to grasp. Make these life skills part of the learning that takes place in your building. Set the bar high when it comes to care for all of humanity and care of the earth. Then sit back and watch your people inspire you. If given positive role modelling, most will reach that high standard when they know someone believes in them. Teaching skills that require honest, open communication, self-awareness and compassionate empathy are foundational skills and tools for students to thrive. Make these pieces part of the day to day interactions in your school setting. Grammar and star constellations are elements of knowledge that can be learned at any age. Human goodness, care and compassion are foundational skills that need to be learned at an early age. Teach life skills, model life skills and celebrate students who display life skills when you see them lived out in your school community. The world needs them.

6. Social-Emotional / Academics: Learning to self-regulate emotions, and learning to express one's needs are skills to be learned. When students are not able to self-regulate and have difficulty saying what they need, it can be difficult to manage a classroom let alone a school setting. Within your particular school community, know the values and tools available to the students that will help them to self-regulate. If something more needs to be implemented, talk to principal colleagues about the methods of self-regulation used in their school settings. Visit other schools and get a sense of the energy and spirit in their buildings. Contact those in your community who are recognized experts in this area around social-emotional behaviour, cultural traditions and differences. Strong school spirit usually indicates a cohesive and positive learning environment for both students and staff. For academics to soar, social-emotional skills need to be in place. Students need effective tools and staff need to believe these are important for the school body.

7. Activity and Intramurals: There are weeks throughout the school year that you will need higher levels of physical activity and more rigid structures to keep students and staff from going off the rails. The two weeks leading up to the major holidays (e.g. Christmas, Spring Break and Summer Holidays) are 'hot' spots for behaviour issues to brew and go sideways. During these weeks, use the 'divide and conquer' strategy in your building. Implement extra lunch intramurals, choir practices, and a variety of 'busy' fillers to keep students moving along. Balance this with a higher level of soothing and calming activities for the students that may already be OVER stimulated by home routines, lack of sleep, or busy schedules. Activities such as puzzles, choir, or knitting clubs can help keep the 'calm'. Learn when more activity is necessary and when calming environments are important in the yearly schedule.

8. Spirit Days: Celebrate Spirit Days during the year as great ways to change the energy in the building. These days are not only for the students, but also for the staff. Events where food can be shared, and groups can perform for the school body, (e.g. choirs, staff vs student sports events, talent shows and plays) are well received and help to celebrate the gifts and talents that are within your school student body. The change of energy in the building is helpful and 'playful' activities help to lighten up both students and staff.

9. Teaching moments: life experiences and community celebrations:
Use the natural rhythm of your school activities as teachable moments. On sports days, talk about the importance of sportsmanship and integrity of athletes. On community event days teach students why Remembrance Day is important and warrants a day off school. Use the time that the school body comes together at assemblies to teach something important that is happening in the school community, local community or global community. Recognize the great things that are happening both in the student body and in your staff's lives (with staff permission). Keep in mind you are a community of learners that grow and enrich each other on a day-to-day basis. This needs to be acknowledged.

10. The community is the classroom: The walls of learning are far beyond the classroom educational systems that are taking place in your building. Make the boundaries for learning far outside the boundaries of your playground. Let the community and outside world be your classroom. Connect with expertise in the community for the drama, art exhibits, sports, trades programs and local SPCA for experiential learning to happen for your students. Budget for fieldtrips, wildlife visits, ecological studies and environmental community learning. Meet with elders in the community; visit the elderly and take a trip to the local waste management plant. Explore with your staff what they are passionate about and give permission for your classes to take adventures and educational trips routinely for advanced learning.

> "If an encouraging, affirming, life-giving environment is what we would expect for our own children, we then need to provide this for the students in our care".

Points to Ponder:
1. What are the educational needs of your students?
2. What are the social-emotional needs of your students?
3. What are the ways you can incorporate community learning into your school routine for instilling the 'community is your classroom' mentality to take place?

Action items:
1. Put on your staff agenda as a discussion topic: "What are you passionate about in the community" and brainstorm ways your classrooms can get out in the community for learning.
2. Visit classrooms and watch your students: what ways do they need to be supported for optimal learning to take place?
3. Talk to teachers and staff. Ask what they need to be able to teach students life skills and what resources do they need to better help them meet academic and social-emotional goals?

Reflections:_____
_____
_____
_____
_____
_____

"Know who You are Agent For" Policy, Procedures, Protocol

"Policies are necessary evils to help schools run consistently and to ensure the health and safety of staff and students. They exist because of possible far-reaching consequences that we may not be able to fathom in our present perspective as principal. Resist the temptation to make exceptions to a policy because of your own (or other staff members') personal feelings in a situation." Laura Lowther

It is important to know who you are 'agent' for as a principal and the mandate and scope of authority you have received. Boards of education, boards of directors, and hierarchical structures exist in your educational system. No matter what your perspectives are about hierarchal structures, the truth of the matter is you work for one. As a principal, it is important for you to read and understand the body of policies, protocols and procedures that exist in your school system. Your school district may use different terminology, but for clarity here, "policies" are created at the level of the school district or diocese and are the backbone, providing a framework that governs all schools. "Protocols" are created at the school council or school board level and they flesh out the particular way these policies are applied according to the unique characteristic of the school. "Procedures" are the step-by-step actions that give tangible evidence that the policy is being lived out. This may not be the same in your structural system however, the following is one example of how this might look:

- Policy (governs all schools): e.g. safety is required in all schools
- Procedures (guidelines specific to site): e.g. mandatory supervision outdoors at the beginning of day 8:15am and end of the day 3:00pm and during all breaks.
- Protocol (step-by-step actions): e.g. use of visi-vests, medical alerts, number of supervisors, set up of playground, etc.

Policy may state you need to provide adequate supervision for your students and staff. Protocols are school specific. Protocols for your students, due to the demographics of your school, may require more supervisors than other schools in your district. Protocols need to be in writing and understood by all in the school community. Principals are responsible for communicating where staff and parents can read these guidelines. Parent handbooks contain the protocols that the school adheres to. Keep your school's protocols current and attainable. Review and date the revisions of protocols every August before the doors of your building open to a new school year. Be careful of "attachment" to certain protocols because 'we have always done it this way'. A new way of doing things can be like 'a breath of fresh air'.

Procedures are the 'how to' routines of the school. These fill staff binders and student codes of conduct. Procedures pertain, for example, to the way you leave the building and which doors are entered or exited after hours. They refer to where students line up in the morning, who the safety personnel on staff are and at what time and what happens in the case of an injury. Procedures need to be clear-cut and known by all staff in your building for the safety of all people. When procedures break down, there is a risk of protocols not being followed and policies being ignored. This can lead to serious situations in schools that can cause harm and lead to further investigations. Be vigilant in keeping procedures concrete, protocols current and accessible, and policies updated and understood.

Read, know and ask questions around policies, procedures and protocols because when you took on the role of principal, you also became the defender of a body of policies and procedures that work together in forming a strong educational institution. They are the legal "line in the sand" that becomes your support and defense when a situation threatens to fall into crisis.

Do not be afraid to ask questions to *'why, what and where'* these policies and procedures originated. Check dates when policies were written. Are they still current, relevant or out of date? Know who has the authority and responsibility to revise a policy or procedure.

When needed, challenge the 'rule makers,' boards and decision-making powers, especially when a policy has an adverse effect on those who have no voice. Keep in mind that what is best for students is at the heart of 'why' policies need to be changed. When revising a policy or procedure, or creating a new one, ensure that all those affected by the policy are taken into account. In the end, 'change for the sake of change' or out of fearful motivation is not helpful and can lead to harm. Rules are meant for helping people to thrive on the path, not to become burdensome on the journey. Keep always at the heart, the people when completing this necessary and important work.

> "One of the most important understandings you need to know as a principal is who you are agent for."

Points to Ponder:

1. Who are the agents that you need to adhere to?
2. What are the policies and protocols that govern your school in the hierarchal system?
3. Where do you find the policies procedures, and protocols of your district/diocese, sister schools and school environment?

Action Items:

- Read the policies that govern your school at the top level.
- Read the parent handbook and the procedures around discipline, code of conduct, and procedures around complaints and emergencies. Never short circuit safety issues or safety procedures. Safety is your number one concern at all times.
- Read and know the staff handbook. Understand updating and revision may be required in consultation with staff and other principal colleagues.

Reflections:_____

_____

_____

"Polite, Positive and Professional" Communication

"No institution can continually improve without an atmosphere of trust, and a desire, individually and collectively, to do better when better is possible. Principals must care about both the individual and the community. Compassion matters." Rosemary McKenzie

Words are an important way of communicating. We need them, we use them, and they flow from our mouth. Verbal or written communication can be both helpful or harmful. Words can be informative or charged with unfiltered emotion. Words are not neutral. There is wisdom in knowing when to hold your tongue or refrain from using written communication. There is prudence in having the right time and place to share what is needed and deemed worthy to share. As principals, either we are using our words consistently or we are having to swallow them and keep our thoughts and verbal responses to ourselves. We use different forms of communication when trying to be positive and encouraging with students, texting a colleague trying to be supportive and honest, or filtering endless communications like emails, memos, agendas and reports where we are to be the voice of truth and reason.

Extroverts will handle their words differently than introverts. Be self-aware. Know yourself and the way people in your building are used to communicating. The receiver interprets and perceives intention once the words are spoken. Perceptions are people's realities. You cannot retract the spoken word. Sometimes our words will be misconstrued. It is part of being human. We are not always going to get it right. Remember people only hear things from where they are at personally and not necessarily what is actually being said. There will be times you will need to repeat and gently remind staff of important information. There will be times you will need to apologise for words spoken whether or not your intentions were meaningful at the time.

Three helpful tools for communication:

1. Be positive: Choose to be affirming and kind. This is definitely a choice that needs to be practiced at times. If you cannot mention a strength or something positive, choose to say nothing but 'thank you for your input'. For some, it will require practice in using helpful words when communicating with others. However, be persistent and patient, it is a learned skill. Learn to smile if it's all you can manage on some days.

2. Be polite: You have no idea what courage it may have taken that parent, staff member, or student to come forward to talk to you. Much of outside circumstances are unknown to principals. Learn from mistakes, and remember parents and others in the community do not have to be professional when they come to talk to you. However, our role and obligation as educators is to always remain professional. By the time the parent has crossed the threshold of your office door to talk about their child around a sensitive issue, chances are they have already had the conversation fifty times in their head. Parents can already be emotional, and they have a preconceived notion of the outcome before entering your office. Listen calmly, affirm and say only what is needed when emotions are high. The higher road is paved with good intentions and kindness; the lower road is gravelled with poor word choices and lack of understanding. Meet with a compassionate heart.

3. Be professional: If you do not want it splashed on a billboard, don't say it, don't write it, and don't document it. Leave it in your head. The written word is never private. Remember that. I believe journal writing is an important reflective tool for principals. However, leave this personal and professional tool at home as a private reflective, processing time.

Keeping words positive, polite, and professional will hold you steadfast. *"Seek to understand,"* a wise colleague once told me. Everyone is walking around with an invisible backpack of pain that is usually unknown to us. A rule of thumb, "Correcting another behind a screen, e.g., email, text or letter, can be an act of cowardice. Share it face to face first." Address issues with a student, staff member or parent by meeting them person to person in a private setting, sharing your feedback gently and with compassion. Positive affirmations can happen through any device, as well as meeting a person face to face. Praise publicly with gratitude and enthusiasm; correct gently with closed door and confidentially.

> "Listen calmly, affirm and say only what is needed. The higher road is paved with good intentions and kindness; the lower road is gravelled with poor word choices and lack of understanding.
> Meet with a compassionate heart".

Points to Ponder:

1. How do I use my words? Ask a trusted friend who knows you well, how your words impact them.
2. Think of someone who used words that affected you positively and note what was said. Note how someone used words to negatively affect you. What was said?
3. What is your preferred way of communicating, e.g. email, letter, face-to-face? How will you communicate with parents, especially the difficult ones?

Action Items:

- Talk with a trusted staff member who understands well the parent culture of the school. What have they observed? Having a general understanding, get involved with the school community. Listen to what is said and watch what is happening.

- Who are your introverts and extroverts on staff? What are you? What does this mean for you and the way you will communicate with your staff?
- Be in attendance as much as possible at Parent Advisory Council meetings and remember to thank them on a continuous basis for their support.
- Have your staff sign a card at Christmas and end of the year for your parent groups. The school newsletter is a great place for words of thanks for all those parents that share time, talent, and treasure with the school community.

Reflections:_____

_____

_____

_____

_____

_____

_____

_____

_____

_____

_____

_____

_____

_____

_____

_____

_____

_____

"Keep Your Own Counsel" Privacy

"Courage does not always roar. Sometimes it is the quiet voice at the end of the day saying 'I will try again tomorrow.'" Irish Proverb

I once knew a principal and deeply admired him as he shared stories of daily experiences regarding his staff and students. Most of what he shared were funny situations or stories of what motivated him to be a better principal. He had a deep respect for his colleagues and staff that he shared his role openly and often reflected with gratitude. However, there were also days when the only thing he had to say was *"The day needs to be taken to the grave."* I knew by his facial expression, body language, and tone that it had been a heavy day. These days seemed to coincide with 'principal's office days.' These were the days he deemed 'the necessary challenges' of his chosen profession where more office conversations would occur, more meetings took place and more policies were in the making. These days were his most challenging.

Parents, teachers and students will share information that knowingly needs to 'start and stop' in your office. There is professional wisdom in this. Discern well what needs to be shared, what can be shared, and what needs to be left on the floor of your office for the custodian to metaphorically 'vacuum up'. You will need to discern for yourself what you will share versus what you will bury. Forming your conscience and being reflective is mandatory in a leadership position. Some situations warrant necessary expertise outside your school will need to be relied on (e.g. social workers, counsellors, police officer school liaison) other times you discern a different approach.

Privacy is a gift all principals need to guard. Having the right to personal information is very different to having the privilege of an individual sharing their personal journey with you. Know the difference between the two. You are human and you are going to make mistakes. However, learn the art of discretion. People who choose to divulge personal information with you need to know you can be trusted. You will need to keep your own counsel and keep the 'rest of the story' to yourself. What your students, parents and other professionals in the school building share with you is confidential. Sometimes you will take the blame for situations and decisions that unfold because you have information that you are not privy to share. Develop a thick skin. At the end of the day, you will need to believe you are doing the best you can at the time, with the information you have at the time. There will be situations where the complainant will only know half the story and you will not be free to share the rest of it. Discretion, privacy, and being a trusted person is a learned practiced skill. Learn it quickly. Value it. Keep it.

> "Know when to keep your own counsel and keep the 'rest of the story' to yourself. Privacy is private. What is told you by students, other parents and other professionals in the building is private."

Points to Ponder:
1. Are you someone who needs to talk and share things about your day-to-day experiences? How strict are you in maintaining confidences? What are the grey areas for you?
2. How aware are you of how your personality type affects your relationships with others? Are you an Extrovert? Introvert? Omnivert? What are the strengths and challenges you face in sharing with others?
3. Do you understand the difference between right to know and need to know? Ask a trusted colleague for examples of both situations that may occur in a school setting.

Action Items:

- Who is a trusted confidant for you?
- Talk with experienced principals. What guidelines do they follow regarding confidences within their school?
- Have a debriefing system that works for yourself. For example, keep a home journal as a way to write out experiences when you cannot share.

Reflections:_____

"Leave a Trail" Document!

"Keeping records can be a two edged sword. Remember that what you write and record may be accessed by people that you may not want to share with. Document for your own protection but do it carefully." Dave Crawley

There will be situations that will require documentation. This is the paper work that may be done long after everyone has gone home or in the early hours of the morning. Here are a few guidelines to keep in mind as you learn your own style of how to keep notes and official documentation.

Five key items in record keeping:

1. A.S.A.P. : As Soon As Possible: When dealing with official documentation in the area of a disclosure, a disciplinary action with staff, a serious intention to harm another by a student to student, or a parental conversation that has gone awry, document as soon as possible. The conversation is fresh, details are still permeating the room, and it is good for you to see clearly what happened in the situation.

2. Write in the third person: When documenting, write in the third person. Keep the documentation factual and objective. Leave subjective language out of the documentation yet state the observable, e.g. "Mrs. ___ appeared to be anxious" or "Mr. __'s voice was loud causing his son to become fidgety and show signs of nervous behaviour." Statements like these can be helpful. When documenting, remember you are the observer-participant. Be clear, concise and to the point.

3. Use and colour code file folders and use a locked cabinet: Keep an 'open' or ongoing file for any serious situation (e.g. social work cases, legal cases etc.) for the duration a student is in your school. A file may become 'open' in kindergarten and may not close until the child leaves the care of your school. When or whether a file can be shredded is dependent upon the policy of your district. Ask superintendents, or experienced principal colleagues if you are unsure, being prudent in your level of sharing information. Be clear in knowing what is done in your school system and how you will deal with situations before they happen.

4. ASK the Superintendent and, as needed, ask for clarification at principals' meetings: When unsure of what to do in situations around documentation, ask those you trust. Principal colleagues and your Superintendent will know procedures around storing documentation. Keep a paper trail. When you get a chance, bring the important topics to face to face principal meetings. Hear what the rest of the principals are doing in regards to record keeping and documentation. This can relieve stress and anxiety around this important and needed task.

5. Help your Teachers: Ensure your teachers are also aware of the importance of documentation. There will be times teachers will be required to document and you will keep records officially in your cabinet. Documenting can be stressful for your teachers, so help create templates for your school which outline key information that needs to be gathered and if possible in the simplest template possible. Review templates before an incident to lessen the anxiety for teachers around documentation. Ask other principals for templates they use.

> "Ask principal colleagues. Shred when appropriate, and be prudent in your level of sharing information."

Points to Ponder:
1. What are the systems for documentation that are already in place in your school?
2. How are you with writing in the third person and being objective?

3. Who are the people that can support you when the time comes that you need to rely on someone?

Action Items:
- Read any 'open' files that are in your school that need your attention.
- Create a system and a place for keeping documentation private and contained.
- Ask your superintendent or another colleague for an example of what correct documentation looks like so you have a sense of what needs to be done when the time comes.

Reflections:_____

"It's NOT in the Manual" Trust Yourself

"When you have a meaningful purpose and a clear vision for your school, making decisions will come with confidence and ease." Katja Groves

Within three minutes on playground duty I ended up on the ground. Walking in winter conditions in Prince George is a slippery slope. As soon as my head hit the frozen earth, I knew this was not going to be pretty. My feet were out from under me in a flash. Before I even had a chance to register mentally what happened, ten kindergarten faces were peering down at me staring in disbelief. "Wow, you okay, Ms. Gilbert?" One offered some helpful advice. "Maybe you need new boots like mine."

There will be many days of slippery slopes. Days when something will happen in a split second and decisions will need to be made immediately; whether it is to do with a disgruntled student that has come through your door or the teacher that needs support with something that could be potentially serious. Sometimes there is no cut and dried discernment process. There will be a patch of uneven terrain forcing you to decide what can be ignored in favour of what needs your attention. There will be situations where you will act and later think better of it. The truth of the matter is sometimes you will just go with common sense, or instinct, and be right. Other times, you may think a situation over from dawn to dusk and still see it go badly.

No matter the situation, no matter how the process finds its resolution, you will need to trust that you did the best you could at the time, with the information you had at the time. You will never be correct 100 percent of the time for all situations. And that is OKAY. There is an expectation that as a principal you are supposed to get it right 100 percent of the time. That's nonsensical. However, nowhere is that expectation more ingrained then in your own mind. Statements such as "I should have known that" or "If only I had that information before making that decision, I could have done that better" are useless. Let those go. What you can trust is that you are imperfect. Slippery slopes will appear at different times on the job. You will fall, people will see, though if you are wise, you will grow and learn from these experiences.

Experience is a great teacher. You get up and trust those around you to have your back. Trust that you will get better at encountering the angry parent, the over tired, hungry student, and the over-stretched, worn out teacher. You will learn how to juggle the demands of paper work, cope with electronic communications and determine what is urgent vs important in your daily routines. You will learn where your strengths are and where you need to grow as an educational leader. You will discover times when the saying "Oh well, we will start again tomorrow" is enough. Trusting yourself and your team will be the greatest gift you can give yourself and the people that surround you. Confidence will grow in you, decisions will come easier as you learn. That first week of school will be chaos. That Christmas concert will be a success, and yes, the end of the year will happen each year, every year. Relax into the rhythm of your building and embrace the moments that fill your day.

> "No matter the situation, no matter how the process sets its resolution, you will need to trust yourself that you did the best you could at the time, with the information you had at the time it was given."

Points to ponder:
1. What strengths do you bring to the role of principal? What do you lack? Are there people who can bring a strength that you do not have? Can you enlist or hire them in some capacity?

2. If you had to choose one area of growth for yourself, what would that be? How might you gain a needed skill or area of expertise?
3. Where is the area that you need to celebrate in your leadership skills? How can you share that beyond the walls of your building?

Action Items:
- If you know of one area that is a 'slippery slope' for you, take a concrete action to help steady the foundation.
- Name one way right now that you can claim as a tool that will help you trust yourself more in your leadership abilities.
- Look at situation that has not worked well, name it and relive the situation with a different strategy where the outcome is more positive and life giving for all parties involved.

Reflections:_____

"The Acorn doesn't Fall Far from the Tree" Parents

'Parents are the primary educators of their children.'
"We need to honour this role of the parents, not just in pamphlets and special events, but in everyday communications and dealings. When we truly see each parent, whatever their circumstance, as equal partners in educating the child, it will strengthen our school community as a whole." Laura Lowther

I have come to believe there are three things that parents want for their children in schools. Parents want to know that their child is *safe*, parents want to know you *know* their child and maybe most importantly that you *care* about their child. I have not met a parent yet that does not love their child and wants the best for them. If parents have concerns about their child of a serious nature, by the time they land at your door they are 'emotional, passionate, and right'. Think about it. You are the last in a chain of people who can 'right what has been wronged' to their child. So expect tension. Expect emotion but expect the parent wants what is best for their son or daughter. The parent may not be professional in their conduct with you, but they don't have to be. Do not be surprised at this. You need to be professional, your staff members need to remain professional, but parents get to be 'passionate'. Moreover, chances are that you will want that. This means they care about their child and that is a good thing. There will be a few parents that will be difficult. They are the ones who take the majority of your time. The time you never seem to have and the energy that you have been saving to pace yourself through the week, that parent *will* land on your doorstep and you will make time and energy for them. While they may be passionate, they must also be respectful.

In difficult situations, no matter how far they are from the truth of what 'really happened with their child', your job as a principal is to 'seek to understand'. Listening is your only avenue in situations like these. Know your frame of understanding, but listen in a way to see the parent's perspective. Parents love their children. I have yet to meet a parent that ultimately is not trying their best for what they think is right for their child. Parents are doing the best they can, with what they have, in the only way they know how. Respect them, affirm them, and help when they ask. The majority of parents are a gift to a school community. Thank them, often.

Four ways parents help build the community:

1. Parent/Family Gatherings: Have family gatherings where parents and students can be together in the school setting. Potlucks, movie nights, and school dances are ways families get to celebrate in the school environment. Provide these events space to happen and get out of the way. These are wonderful events that bring families together and are led by parents themselves. Step back and support the information that needs to be communicated, but understand these can be parents' initiatives led by parent groups. Pop in if needed, but make yourself scarce. Let the parents take ownership of many of these events outside school hours. If the interest is there, encourage teachers that are passionate about these events to take part. You as principal choose wisely where and when you go to these events.

2. Expertise in your parents: Parents come with a variety of gifts and talents that they can offer the school community. Invite parents to make known the skills they have that can benefit your school, and how they may be called upon to contribute to the school community. As a need arises, personally invite parents to contribute. Encourage, be enthusiastic about initiatives and invite gently.

3. School councils and boards: Build your councils and boards with positive, professional, and varied parents. Every parent wants the best for their child. Ask for help when you need it. Appreciate your parent helpers every chance you get. Answer questions openly and be transparent about the happenings that are taking place in your building. Better they hear information from you than from their child when they get home from school. Communicate with parents and keep them informed.

4. Boundaries: Set clear boundaries around your relationship with parents. You are in a professional role. There are times when lines of friendship may get blurred, especially if communities are closely knit. You and your staff will find yourselves working with the same family for many years when there is more than one child in the school. However, be vigilant in remembering your role and have your own expectations around parents. You do not have to be at everything that the Parent Advisory Group puts on. Know your boundaries, and remind staff of their boundaries as professionals. Learn to walk away from sensitive conversations and stop conversations in the community that would be better shared in your school office.

> "Parents are doing the best they can, with what they have, in the only way they know how. Respect them, affirm them, and help when they ask".

Points to Ponder:
1. Reflect on how you communicate with parents. Where are your strengths and weaknesses as a school leader when meeting with parents?
2. What does the parent encounter teach me about their family, their child and their living environment? How can I support their family?
3. What do parent meetings teach me about myself? What do I experience rising up in me before, during and after a parent meeting? Note this. It is awareness that can help you as you encounter more and more parent meetings.

Action Items:

- Share with parents the great things that are happening with their child, especially the ones who you know are strugglers. Shine a bright light on a success you witnessed or were informed of by a staff member. If the principal is celebrating it, it adds power to the celebration.
- Have a list made of all parental volunteers in your school community. At Christmas and end of school year write a Christmas 'Thank You' letter that is mailed home or via 'backpack express'. Gratitude has a powerful effect.
- Have a column in the monthly school newsletter just for 'thanking' parents that have helped in the school that month. This is a great space to also request volunteers for upcoming events and school tasks.
- Remind staff about the importance of polite, positive, and professional relationships with parents. Consistent boundaries and gentle reminders are necessary from you as a leader in the school.

Reflections_____

_____

_____

_____

_____

_____

_____

_____

_____

_____

_____

_____

"Who's Free for Breakfast?" Collective Wisdom

"Every principal needs a support system, a sounding board, someone to break bread with. Take advantage of colleagues and mentors who have experience and wisdom gained over the years. Important decisions have to be considered carefully – take the time to get input from those you trust and respect." Dave Crawley

There are never enough hours in the day to do what needs to be done as a principal. The meetings, emails, and phone calls to return will be endless. Expect it, know it, prioritize and make time for what needs to be done. No two days are ever the same in your role as principal, and one of the beautiful benefits of this position is that it keeps you alive, on your toes and moving. However, the one factor to keep forefront is, never miss meetings when there is collective wisdom to be shared face-to-face. You do not, will not, and cannot have all the answers alone. Work in collaboration with others and ask for input. Opportunities for collective meetings with other principals are essential and necessary. Know your trusted colleagues and then 'ask, seek and share' your concerns for your people. This allows for a fresh set of ears to listen and share supportive advice, correct you gently and give you an idea you may have missed.

Colleagues may have insight that will benefit your people that you may not have ever considered. The end decision will still be yours and you will need to own that, however, collective wisdom is like a path already paved before you. The greatest asset of being part of a collaborative group is knowing that, at some stage, there is no situation that has not occurred before, there is no principal that is left unscarred, and there is no principal that doesn't have the heart for their people if they stay in the vocation long enough. Some meetings will leave you refreshed, renewed and recharged while others will leave you pondering, questioning, and seeking to understand. Either way you are being stretched or propelled forward in the decision-making process for your school. Know you need these meetings for your professional journey. Some collective wisdom sharing may take place in the pub, the breakfast hour, or later in the evening beyond the hours of a school day.

Whatever setting your gathering holds, have food, beverages, and a private space to dialogue well, and listen well. When needed, use an agenda where important current issues can be brought to the table that hold greater importance than other issues. Make time in the agenda to hear from all the people in the group so all get a chance for 'air time.' If people take time to show up for the meeting, have the courtesy to hear the views and perspectives of all who gather – even if at times you feel you have to dig deep for the pearl. All people in the meeting have something to offer.

Four items to note when gathering for a meeting:
(Applicable to many types of meetings)

1. In control vs in charge: There is a difference between being 'in control' of the conversation and being 'in charge' of the conversation. 'In control' is micro-managing and manipulating a certain outcome in a conversation. This is not helpful for the growth of the whole, if one's mindset is rigid and closed. Being 'in charge' of the gathering means taking responsibility to ensure an agenda is prepared and that the conversation stays respectful and in everyone's best interest. All items may not be accomplished, however, everyone needs a chance to share safely. Be ready to explore alternative avenues and ideas that may be brought to the table. For people to share genuinely and honestly, there needs to be a space of trust, and mutual respect that is at the foundation of the meeting. Do not be afraid to start meetings reminding others of this important basic stance of trust and basic norms in your gathering, especially if new people are joining or there are sensitive matters to discuss.

2. Know when to unplug: Having your eyes, ears and personal energy constantly linked to technology is not beneficial for you. Take a break from it. When gathering for a face-to-face meeting refrain from using any form of technology. Ideally, use paper and pen instead of laptops, and remind everyone present that cell phones are to be turned off and put away in pockets or briefcases. If the meeting is to last longer than three hours, set times during the meeting when people can check their devices. Anything shorter than 3 hours- the outside world can survive without you. The people you are meeting with should be your top priority and deserve your full attention because they are the ones who made the effort to show up.

3. Communications: Written notes or minutes are a vital part of a meeting. You will not remember everything so do not trust everything to memory. Written minutes, for example, document changes that have been made to policies and to procedures. They show a level of transparency in how something was handled and capture creative ideas that you may want to integrate into your own school.

4. Read the people: Learn to read body language and understand non-verbal cues. If conversation has stopped mid-meeting, maybe you have gone too long or people have shut down because of a sensitive topic. No matter what the situation, remember people will not appreciate being called to a meeting that they do not find helpful. A wise principal once shared, know when to halt a meeting, postpone a meeting, or handle an agenda item through a written memo if it's information sharing and do not waste the personal time of your staff. Distinguish agenda items of information from items that need discussion. The items on the agenda need to be of concern to the participants. Many business leaders will say that if there is little positive engagement from the participants in the first 15 minutes, there is something in the space that needs to be attended to before the meeting can be productive.

> "Meetings with colleagues will leave you richer in knowledge and wisdom than when you first arrived."

Points to Ponder:
1. When was the last time you asked your colleagues for a gathering?
2. Who are the wisdom providers in your profession?
3. Where do you go to seek your own inner wisdom?

Action Items:
- Create a list of those that you will turn to who are further along the professional journey. What are the gifts they offer? Tell them.
- What resources will you gather and provide to guide your staff and teachers for their own professional development?
- What are the protocols around technology in your building that serve you for the betterment of personal connection in your school? Communicate that to staff so the boundaries are clear in meetings, on school grounds and during their professional workday.

Reflections:_____

_____
_____
_____
_____
_____
_____
_____
_____
_____
_____
_____

"Thank Them, Feed Them, Celebrate Them" Staff

"It is important to lead, however; whether it is the front of your team or behind your team, it must always be done with the students' best interest in mind." Brent Arsenault

A principal I admired and knew well had this motto: T.E.A.M. – Together Everyone Achieves More. He did not coin the phrase, but he used it like a mantra in many facets of his life. Both in his personal and professional life he exemplified the T.E.A.M. philosophy. Having a motto you are known for can be a powerful and important echo of your personal ethos. For this particular principal, T.E.A.M. spoke widely to many situations and ways of handling school circumstances that arose.

As principals leading a body of people, you need a team. You are only as strong and effective as those that fill your buildings and are willing to dedicate themselves to the same principles, vision and values that you claim as your own in your school. Moreover, you can only move at a pace that your team is willing to move, strive and commit to, together.

Your team of people consists of all the individuals that work under your leadership. The custodian, the maintenance person, bookkeeper and even the spare secretary on call are part of your team. Do not overlook anyone. Know your key people. Know your spare people. Know those that remain on the sideline waiting for you to call upon them. Those who may not be team players are the ones where your 'arms of compassion' need to be wider and greater. Appreciate your TEAM. You will need to work with a variety of people. It does not matter if the contribution made by the individual is great or small to the running of your building. It is a gift that person is offering and without it your school would be less. Honour and treat all offerings, as generous gift, and your school will be a place of celebration.

Here are twelve ways to support your staff:

1. *Champion your staff:* Make staff achievements great. Celebrate and support positive initiatives that help the school move forward and grow.
2. *Professional Development:* You are the main educational leader in your school. Keep your staff learning. To do this often means you will need to keep learning yourself. The best teachers are the best students. Be willing to be stretched and keep stretching those in your charge. You have an obligation to provide the best education for students and staff. Plan quality professional development for your staff members.
3. *Help staff to discover their passion:* All people have secret yearnings and talents yet to be explored. Help your people discover what is great inside them that is often hidden in the busyness of the work day.
4. *Make sure your staff know you are in it with them:* Don't expect anything from your people that you are not willing to do yourself. Be willing to pick up the mop, clean up after a sick child, unplug a toilet or shovel out the entranceways. Take the duty shift, run a PE class, or supervise bus lines. Be part of what your teachers are part of everyday.
5. *Staff members have lives outside of school:* Support your people in what is important to them and help them maintain life balance professionally and personally. Healthy staff make for healthy students. Provide healthy treats in the staff room.
6. *Encourage health:* Support all staff to take their wellness days and encourage healthy lives. Model healthy initiatives in your school.
7. *Affirm, appreciate, and advocate for your staff:* Check in with your staff often and regularly. Share what you notice in positive ways and stand up for your people.

Affirm great things that are happening in your building. Appreciate the time and effort your staff are making and advocate for those staff members that want to try new initiatives, continue educational degrees and are involved in positive ways in the community.

8. *Be brave and humble:* Have the courageous conversations required as a leader. There will be times you will need to deal with uncomfortable situations, be brave. Mix bravery and humility and use the two equally. Acting with humility is knowing you are only where you are by the grace of others, working with others and not entirely from your own endeavours.

9. *Learn from your people*: Look, listen, see what is happening. All have something to teach you. Your staff and students are your teachers. Learn from them.

10. *Trust body language over words.* The body talk is greater than what the mouth is saying. Body language, well understood, will not lead you astray. Pay attention to what is before you and what is being communicated. Be sensitive to cultural differences that could be misread, e.g. in some cultures not engaging in eye contact is a sign of respect for an elder and not an effort to hide something.

11. *Hire those that are NOT YOU:* Interview and hire staff that are going to balance out your school expertise, educational background and energy level. Include teachers that have a variety of gifts to make the work place grow. Be a visionary when staff planning. Hire staff that can contribute that which in humility, you know are not your gifts.

12. *Say THANK YOU, show THANK YOU and live THANK YOU:* Shower your staff with affirming words, hand written cards, treats, tokens and check-ins on a regular basis throughout the year.

> "As principals leading a body of people, you need a team. You are only as strong and as effective as your team."

Points to Ponder:

1. Your staff will do what you are willing to do. What will you do for your staff and what are you not willing to do?
2. Who are the staff that are team players and who are not? Know them and work with them. Most school staffs have mentor teachers, know which are yours.
3. What are the leadership skills of those that may not be teacher leaders? How can you get them to lead with passion for what has heart and meaning for them?

Action Items:

- Schedule intentional times of the year you are going to celebrate your staff: Thanksgiving, Christmas, Spring Break. Write them in your calendar. Write your staff note cards, or put treats in their mailboxes to say 'Thank You' for being part of the TEAM.
- At the next assembly or celebration, publicly affirm your staff in front of the students. It is important for the students to know how proud you are of your TEAM and it is very important for your TEAM to know that you have their backs.
- At the start and end of each year, schedule one-on-one meetings with all your staff as a way to to affirm, congratulate and support face-to-face your TEAM players.

Reflections:_____

_____
_____
_____
_____
_____
_____

"Hiring, Mentoring and Resignations" Educational Leadership

"You need to hire first and foremost caring, compassionate people who are flexible individuals who excel and are dedicated to the art of teaching."
Brent Arsenault

Hiring, mentoring and accepting the resignation of teachers is one of the most important aspects of your role. We all want good people working in our school community and teaching our students. This is a time consuming, all-encompassing, important work that will shape your current staff, impact your students and form school culture. Take the time needed for this process to be completed well and take this task seriously.

Hiring: If you are directly responsible for hiring teachers for your school be well informed. Read resumés, portfolios and letters of referral, follow-up with reference checks, and have an initial conversation with a potential hire outlining what specific characteristic about the school or position the person needs to know. If the hiring of teachers is not in your hands, find ways you can have input to the people who are hiring for your school so you can receive the best fit for what you are looking for in a professional. Once the teacher is in your building, then the moulding and shaping is yours. Choosing the right character fit is the foundation from which you will build.

Mentoring: Mentoring novice teachers is an important aspect in all educational leadership. I have come to understand this area is best done collectively by mentor teachers and principal together. The more gifts and talents that can be shared with novice teachers the better. Talk with trusted mentor teachers and ask for help in this area. From my experience, I have learned I do not have to be strong at all strands of the educational process and subject areas, however I am responsible for finding the best person available for my teachers to learn from, whether a mentor teacher or an expert outside the school. It is my responsibility to bring in and provide the resource person, space and professional development time for my teachers to attain a needed component in their ongoing development. I have come to trust that people know deep down what they need if given the time to reflect and articulate areas for professional growth. Whether it is the novice teacher wanting help with setting up the classroom, the mediocre teacher needing inspiration and resources, or the mentor teacher needing a day with outside professionals. When asked with genuine interest, staff will share what they need to make their learning environment stronger, more current and innovative for students and school colleagues.

Resignations: Teachers will leave your building from resignations. I found this a most difficult moment the first time it happened at my school. I felt like I failed this person. I felt uncomfortable, awkward and unprepared to hear the news when a teacher came to share that they were leaving. However, after talking to other principal colleagues and listening to shared experiences I have found peace with these situations. For me, the best avenue to take when staff decide to move on is to bless them and let go. In blessing the staff member you get to affirm them, celebrate what can be an already stressful decision for the staff member and encourage the journey they are willing to take outside your doors. Take time to thank and affirm the staff member for the time and commitment they have given to the school community and let them leave your office feeling taller in their accomplishments than when they first arrived to your office to share the news. Losing a teacher that has impacted your students and community in a positive way is a gift that you have been given. We do not seize and own our people, but receive our team for the time they are meant to be with us on the journey. Bless the ones that leave, and let go.

Five helpful items in educational leadership

1. *Do not go it alone:* Seek and find educational leaders in and outside your building that you need to make curriculum and instruction better in your school. Find what works for other schools. Research what is working from other outside sources and

experts. Reflect on what would be best for your school and talk with those that are in the classrooms as to what they think is best for the students. Learn from as many outside sources as possible before deciding internally what needs to be provided for your staff and students. In the end, listen to your staff in final decision making.

2. *Provide Professional Development that is current and innovative:* As an educational leader you know the educational system is always changing, growing and in flux. Know the teaching practices of the people in your school and invite and encourage new and exciting ways that are practical for your staff and students. If your school does not have the resources for latest technology, ask the experts what will work for your school, still providing the educational opportunities you need for your students. Do not be afraid to ask and seek as many opinions as needed for you to make an informed choice for your school community.

3. *Ministry guidelines and updates:* Regularly visit the Ministry of Education website and read any updates that post for your province. Make time to learn about the initiatives and resources the Ministry of Education provides for schools. This kind of reading will keep you current and updated, knowing the latest and greatest that is happening in the province. This is a mandatory part of your profession.

4. *Respect and honour the novice and mentor teachers in your buildings:* Teachers come with all sorts of stories, experiences and backgrounds. Novice teachers are cognisant of the most current educational practices and have an enthusiasm for the teaching profession. Mentor teachers have the experience and wisdom of what is tried and true. Meshing these two ways of teaching is both important and needed in a school community. Honour where each teacher is at, while at the same time invite them to reflect on where they feel the need to be stretched.

5. *The best teachers are the best students:* Keep everyone learning. Whether through resources of literature, educational resources or collaborative meetings, keep your teachers growing and learning. When the educators in your school are no longer

taking their professional development seriously, that is a sign that the staff has become stagnant and change is needed. Do not assume that you as principal know what your people need; ask them and then provide what they need to start learning again. When you see grants available, apply for them. Often extra monies coming into the school can ignite creativity, imagination and new learning and teaching opportunities to happen in the school building. Look for where money might be available for new initiatives.

> "In the area of professional development, I have found the best line that has held me steadfast is asking 'What do you need?'"

Points to Ponder:
1. How comfortable are you in mentoring your novice teachers?
2. Who are the experts inside and outside your building that you will turn to?
3. What are the areas you as a principal need to grow in order to create the best educational environment possible for your staff and students?

Action Items:
- Contact other principals in your district about resources and experts available in the community.
- Make a list of resource people and ministry of education websites that will be needed in your role as principal.
- Talk to mentor teachers you trust and invite them to help mentor a novice teacher that is new to your building. What can you learn from your novice teachers?

Reflection:_____
_____
_____

"Standing On the Shoulders of Giants" Role of the Elders

"Great leaders inspire and foster growth in others by building and nurturing relationships steeped in mutual trust and respect." Tamara Berg

If knowledge is power, experience is golden. The more time you take listening to experiences and personal stories the better equipped you will be in your role. Listen and invite people's experiences. There is a sacred history of the giants who walked and worked in the halls before you. There is a trust and respect that's shared when honouring and knowing the past. Learn from mentor teachers and past council and board members. Share with novice teachers and new board members the history of the school in which they now are a part. It is crucial for collective understanding to know where the school has been in order to plan where you want to go.

Hearing stories of the past gives you an opportunity to acknowledge other's feelings, experiences, and contributions made. Great leaders have gone before you. Hearing other's stories are a way of building trust and respect in the community. Everyone has something to share and experiences may be wide and varied. People want to tell their story. Listen with acceptance, be non-judgemental and express gratitude for the gift offered in the sharing. Take note of the personal investment and commitment of staff members, whether it is your secretary or the educational assistant that has dedicated the last ten or fifteen years of their life to the school.

Ponder those that have spent years building what you now enjoy and work in. Invite the elders into your school to talk to students and staff. Before you make changes, hear the struggles and triumphs that took place when the playground was built, the new classrooms were added or the gym paint colour was chosen. Keep in mind the smallest changes will affect someone and will cause a ripple. Where will those ripples end up? Even if a change is for the good, be sensitive to those the change will impact and change slowly. It must be kept in mind, however, that sometimes the circumstances dictate that a change needs to happen quickly, e.g. in matters of safety.

Some schools have found it helpful to dedicate rooms, awards and special spaces in a school building to people who have worked and made significant differences in the school community. Dedicating rooms in a school is a significant way to give special tribute to those that have paved the path before you on the school's journey. Moreover, knowing the history may be important simply so the mistakes of the past are not repeated. Likewise, new initiatives can be brought forward with hope and positive receptivity for those that will benefit from the change.

> "When taking the 'helm' of any school it is important to know its history."

Points to ponder:
1. Who are the people in your building that are able to share their story about the history of your school?
2. Where would you find information about the important milestones of your school in the local community?
3. Who are the 'giants that have gone before you' who made the school what it is today? Can you acknowledge them in some way through dedications or special ceremonies?

Action Items:
- Take time to talk with one person who knows the history of your school.
- Take time to look at photos, files, and reports from past principals.
- Schedule times in your school year to have community people come to talk to students about the history of the school.

- Alumni, past teachers, and prominent community members love to share their story at graduations and other events. Invite the people of past generations to share their story.

Reflections: _____
_____
_____
_____
_____
_____
_____
_____
_____
_____
_____
_____
_____
_____
_____
_____
_____
_____
_____
_____
_____

"Let Us Pray" Faith Based Schools

Faith based education nurtures the whole student by encouraging each child to grow beyond academics. Faith based schools provide an environment in which shared values of morals and spirituality are supported by principals, teachers and staff. The teachings of faith can be heard and felt from each classroom to the far end of the playground."
Katja Groves

I am grateful that I work in a faith-based school system. At their best, they are unique and holistic places where spirit can freely flow through expressions of faith. They value rituals that express and deepen one's experience of the mysteries of human life, e.g. birth, death, forgiveness, and traditions. In these schools, the common good is a foundational starting point. Prayer is not simply rote or routine, but becomes a vital and public element expressing an integrated way of life. Faith will be the lens from which all subject areas will be taught, a place of refuge in times of crisis, and will become, if not already, the energy that will lead, surround and call forth the gifts and talents of staff and students. Be PROUD you lead a faith-based school. Make God the priority. Never apologise for it, and trust and rely on the given grace that comes with the profession of leading a faith based school.

Faith based schools take their place rightly alongside secular schools. We need both. We need the tensions and support of both systems. Learn to work together and when possible support each other with communications around transferring students and other issues of mutual concern for the betterment of the local families. If you are a faith based school you will rely at times on the secular schools as students will flow between both systems.

Be aware of the ebb and flow of each system and remember at the end of the day the focus is what is best for the students that come to your door.

Three intentional items when leading a faith-based school

1. Celebrate: No matter what the tradition of faith is in your school, remember to celebrate it often. Refer to it daily and start with a simple ritual at each meeting or gathering, whether with staff or with students. Role modelling celebrations reinforces the practices parents want for their children or they wouldn't have come to your school door.

2. Know the core virtues: The core virtues of faith-based school e.g. respect, kindness, forgiveness, love, and service need to be learned, taught and celebrated with staff and students. You as principal need to know, practice and understand the lens of faith from which you lead. There will be times when you will lead the assemblies, prayer liturgies, and celebrate memorable moments like staff baby showers, or grandparent's funerals in your community. Know the language common to your faith-based schools.

3. It's a never ending journey: Remember that all people are on their own journey and will walk the path at their speed in their own time. Having a level of expectation for faith development and teaching of students needs to be the basic level of understanding between principal and staff. However, it has to be an area that you as a leader are acquainted with, understand and are comfortable sharing with teachers and staff. At the same time, as you model for your school community the best you can, remember the journey is long and never finished until the end of our time on this earthly journey. Trust and rely on the source of all Life as you understand and believe in it. Make your faith journey a priority in your life.

> "Faith will be the lens through which all subject areas will be taught; a place of refuge in times of crisis, and will become if not already the energy that will lead, surround and call forth the gifts and talents of staff and students."

Points to Ponder:
1. How would you describe your personal relationship with the Creator?
2. How much time and energy do you invest in this part of your life?
3. How comfortable are you in leading prayer for your students and staff?

Action Items:
- Meet and learn from your mentor teachers that have lead prayer celebrations. What has been done in the past that are held as sacred celebrations in the school community?
- What are the resources used in the school for prayer, liturgies and celebrations? Find them and read them. Dialogue with other principals what they are using in their schools.
- Determine what you need to deepen your own understanding and appreciation for your faith and search out the resources (e.g. courses, retreats, reading) that will contribute to your learning.
- Walk your school building and look for signs that you are a faith-based school. What are the symbols, sayings, and inspiring examples that decorate your walls, bulletin boards and entry-ways?

Reflections:_____
_____
_____
_____

"Tapping Out" What will You Leave Behind?

"I've cherished each and every day that I've been in principalship. So much of my year was spent reflecting and planning ahead. As I retire, it is difficult to jump off the merry-go-round and land on my feet." Dave Crawley

I am not one for contact sports. However, I have been in a boxing ring a time or two. An athlete engaged in this enclosed ring contact sport learns quickly when it's time to 'tap out'. Tapping out is knowing when you are finished and need to get out. Tapping out happens at the end of the day, the week or the end of your time in your school. You recognize that you have done all you can do physically, emotionally or mentally, and will start again tomorrow. I have found helpful at the end of the day to look at the next day's agenda, make a list of what are key items needing to be addressed and then leave the building. Let go of the day as you leave the building. I have this same routine and ritual entering the building and exiting the building on any given day. This keeps me grounded in how I will face the challenges and delights of the day.

However, tapping out is also significant when you know in your inner being that it is time to bring closure to the current principal position or your career. If you are closing your professional role in your school community there will come a time when you realize you have done enough. Part of taking on any profession is having the wisdom to know when to 'tap out'. There will come a time when you will know it is time to leave and pass the 'keys on to the next guardian'. Most often, the circumstances around your departure will be yours alone. Your heart will know its own time. Take time with this decision-making process and discern the timing well.

There are a few areas you will need to consider as you ponder leaving this position, e.g. timing of the announcement, what needs to be completed before the next hire, how to communicate with staff and parents, etc. Make lists and set a plan. Once the announcement has been made, one third of the people affected will be sad you are leaving, one third will delight in the fact, and one third will not give you a second thought. Trust the natural transferring process. Trust your people to help you in the last chapter of your role as principal so you may live it out well. Work hard until the last day and be the best you can be for those that have placed their trust in you.

Five important items to remember when getting ready to 'tap out':

1. Train well for the passing of the guard: Leave the next person in charge the best possible advice and assistance you can offer. Put in place what you can as stepping stones for the next person at the 'helm'. Do the best you can to ensure that they will succeed. Prepare your staff, leave a healthy budget when possible and prepare your school families to welcome the next principal with open arms.

2. Leaving the legacy: What will be your legacy when you walk out the door? Will your legacy be a positive one of encouragement? Have you left your building better than you found it? More importantly, have you left your students, families and staff better than you found them?

3. Thank your people: You did not do anything by your own steam, grace or willpower. Every part of a school is work done collaboratively. Thank those that have been with you on the journey. Especially those that have challenged, stretched and invited you to be MORE than you ever thought you could be. Leave a spirit of gratitude as you leave your office, building and playground on that final day.

4. Intentional pause: Take time for reflection. Take the time to pause and evaluate how your time was spent during your work, effort and role as principal. It is never easy taking the time for reflection because it takes just that: TIME. There are always highs and lows to every life well lived. The need for this intentional pause will allow time for you to settle and let go of that which you do not want to bring forward into the next chapter of your life.

5. Gratitude: Give thanks for being able to be of service, for leaving imprints on people's lives, and being involved in a profession that makes a difference in people's lives. You were given the gift of forming lives, rubbing shoulders with dedicated people, and an opportunity to share talents you didn't know you had. Give Thanks!

> "Depending on the circumstances and the journey you have had and relationships you have built with your people, try your best to leave well."

Points to Ponder:
1. How will you 'tap out' at the end of the day?
2. Talk to a trusted colleague about your 'tapping out' exit plan when the time comes.
3. When you know it is time to leave your profession, what are you leaving for the next principal to inherit?
4. What is the legacy you will leave behind? Be honest with yourself.

Action Items:
- What needs to be shredded VS shared in the handing over the 'Keys to the Castle?' How will you close well?
- Have courageous conversations with those that need it before bringing to completion your role as principal. What needs to be acknowledged or completed before you can walk away in peace?
- Make a gratitude list of all the people that have helped your journey while in this role. Share words of thanks to each person whether in a letter, phone call, email or in public gratitude at a closing event.

Reflections:

Keep Moving Forward… From the Superintendent of CISPG: I am blessed to work with the contributors of this book who are dynamic, Catholic, faith filled educational leaders and who demonstrate the proven essentials of effective leadership: to Listen, Dream, Laugh, Affirm, and Pray. Our shared work is to continually nurture, challenge and grow great Catholic leaders in education at all levels so that we have vibrant Catholic learning communities. Often, it means taking the time to reflect, write and share our insights like our author has encouraged us to do as current leaders of our schools.

Complementing the great insights already written by the author, here are a few items that have served me well in my leadership roles. I hope they are helpful to you.

1. Start each day, meeting and meal with prayer. You never know the impact you have on a person or group of people gathered and that potential is both frightening and awesome.

2. No matter how choppy the water, always do 'the next right thing'. We are not perfect and we learn from our choices. Admitting mistakes will help us realize our full potential and demonstrate integrity and faithful commitment.

3. Strong Arts = Strong schools and communities. Do NOT cut the ARTS when resources are tight – rather, recruit dynamic people to lead the music, drama, dance and visual arts. Kids taking part in the Arts is some of the most inspiring and amazing work we do in education.

4. Ensure that students are as curious when they leave our school as when they began. If you forget what that curiosity is, walk back down to the kindergarten room.

5. The students that challenge us, are often the ones remembered the most later in our career because they helped us grow the most – true story.

6. At times the 'YES' to Catholic education is tough. However, being a leader in Catholic education is truly purposeful and very rewarding work. 'Cast your cares on the Lord and He will sustain you.' Psalm 55:22

Humbly,
Chris Dugdale,
Fellow Lifelong Learner.

After thoughts from the Author...

This concise handbook is written within the context of my personal lived experience and what I hold as important threads of my professional and personal journey. So glean whatever kernels may contribute to your growth as a more reflective, intentional and creative educational leader. Let the rest fall behind you like chaff in the wind.

There is one topic, however, I have not mentioned that needs to be addressed if only in a cursory way. It is the whole dimension of YOU, as a principal, staying well, balanced and healthy when taking on and living fully this role of principalship.

A wise friend gently reminds me time and time again of the airline protocol when flying on an airplane: *"Put on your own oxygen mask first before assisting another person"*. This good friend shares this in gentle kindness as a reminder of the importance of self-care. Teasing perhaps, but making a valid point that when I find myself worn out and weary from caring for others, at some stage I have stopped taking care of myself. Taking care of oneself, wrapped in the preverbal truth that "you can't give to another what you do not possess yourself," is an area of your life you need to take seriously. Whether you need to schedule additional time with loved ones, add energy-building exercises in your day like the physical pursuits you enjoy, or maintain healthy personal connections that help your spirit soar, be intentional with your own self-care. No matter what it is that makes your heart sing, include these in your week. Honour those activities, appreciate them and enter fully into the life-giving opportunities they provide to keep you healthy. If we as leaders are not taking care of ourselves, focusing attention on being well, balanced and healthy, then we cannot help those around us to do the same, and we will not lead and guide to our true potential.

Keep on, Keeping on...

Rebecca

Acknowledgements

Many thanks to all who took time to read and encourage this Principals' Handbook.

To Patti, Josephine and Marie for your words of encouragement.

To Susan who took hours over three days doing the 'open heart surgery' on the final draft.

I am so grateful to all of you for your support, affirmation and expertise.

Your friendships are such a gift to me.

Contributors to the Principals' Handbook

Brent Arsenault is in his thirteenth year as principal of St. Mary's School, Prince George B.C. He has taught from grades two to grade twelve in both the public and the Catholic school system in British Columbia and Alberta. Mr. Arsenault received his Masters in Leadership and Administration from Gonzaga University in 2007. He is an avid hockey coach as well who has coached both full and part-time with many junior hockey organizations. Mr. Arsenault loves reading about leadership styles and has a passion for working with children.

Tamara Berg is in her first year as principal of Veritas School, where she taught for three years in addition to teaching for many years in Alberta and British Columbia. She is currently completing her Masters in Educational Leadership. Mrs. Berg is passionate about ensuring students feel boundless in their learning and experience positive learning environments. She is blessed to have a supportive husband and three wonderful daughters.

Dave Crawley has been a teacher, coach, and parent for forty years. This journey started at Thornhill Junior Secondary in Terrace in 1976, with an assignment in English, Socials, and Counselling. Mr. Crawley has been a department head of student services, a district elementary counsellor, principal of four elementary schools and vice-principal and principal of a large student junior high school. Mr. Crawley was the principal of Veritas Catholic School in Terrace for five years.

Chris Dugdale is the Superintendent of eight Catholic Schools in the Diocese of Prince George. He has a wealth of experience as a principal, teacher and coach. He brought this expertise to the Catholic Independent School system five years ago. Chris is a passionate family man and believes in 'doing the next right thing'. Mr. Dugdale enjoys the outdoors hunting and fishing with family and friends.

Katja Groves is a principal at St. Anthony's school in Kitimat, B.C.
She is passionate about the success of not only her students and staff but to providing a faith based school that is welcoming to all families. Ms. Groves strongly feels that providing children with a Catholic Education as a gift that will last a life time. Ms. Groves has been dedicated to Catholic Education for the past twelve years and has recently completed her Masters in Arts Leadership at Royal Roads University.

Terri Haynal's teaching career and principalship started in 1998 at Notre Dame School in Dawson Creek. She has never looked back. Born and raised in Saskatchewan, living in Northern B.C. has always been like home. Mrs. Haynal finds the future so exciting in an ever-changing world. Her motto: Practice reckless optimism! Mrs. Haynal is an advocate for the students and families that attend her school in the community of Dawson Creek.

Laura Lowther is in her ninth year as Principal of Annunciation School. Laura was born and raised in the beautiful coastal town of Prince Rupert, B.C. Her favourite place to be is at home with a good book, or out along the waterfront for a walk with her kids. Mrs. Lowther loves to host family gatherings when everyone arrives with armfuls of food and loud energy.

Rosemary A. McKenzie has been a learner, educator and principal her whole life. However, being a parent is the single greatest role for her. Mrs. McKenzie finds that parenthood is the most important, most humbling, and most meaningful aspect of her life. Mrs. McKenzie has been a principal for eleven years at two separate times at St. Joseph's School in Smithers, B.C. Her school is Kindergarten to grade seven.

Donncha O'Callaghan is a principal in his thirteenth year at Immaculate Conception School, Prince George B.C. He began his teaching career in Cork, Ireland in 1986 before emigrating to Canada in 1991. Since coming to this part of the world, Mr. O'Callaghan has taught up to grade nine in various Catholic school systems in British Columbia and Alberta. He received his Masters in Leadership and Administration from Gonzaga University in 2007. He is a lifelong learner who has never lost his passion for working with children.

Leadership and Professional Resource List

Burgess, D. (2012). *Teach Like A Pirate: Increase Student Engagement, Boost Your Creativity and Transform Your Life as an Educator.* Dave Burgess Consulting. CA., USA.

Caine, G & Caine. R, et all. (2005). *12 Brain/ Mind Learning Principles in Action.* Sage Publication. California, USA.

Canadian Catholic School Trustees Association. (2002). *Build Bethlehem Everywhere.* Toronto, Ontario. Canada.

Covey, S. (1990). *The Seven Habits of Highly Effective People.* Simon and Schuster, New York, USA.

Conyers, M. & Wilson, D. (2015). *Positively Smarter: Science and Strategies for increasing Happiness, Achievement and Well-Being.* Wiley-Blackwell. MA., USA.

Couros, G. (2015). *The Innovators Mindset: Empower Learning, Unleash Talent, and Lead a Culture of Creativity.* Dave Burgess Consulting, Inc., CA., USA.

Douglas, P. (2012). *Time-Style: Style-Based Tools for Managing Priorities, Projects and Deadlines.* P.A. Douglas and Assoc. WA., USA.

Dweck, C. (2nd Ed. 2016). *Mindset. The New Psychology of Success.* Random House LLC, New York., USA.

Eppley, H. & Melander, R. (2002). *The Spiritual Leaders Care to Self-Care.* Alban Institute Publication.

Goleman, D. & Druker, P, et all. Harvard Business Review (2011). *On Leadership.* Harvard Business Review Press, Boston Massachusetts, USA.

Hahn, T. (2011). *Planting Seeds: practicing mindfulness with children.* Parallax Press, USA.

Hawn, G. (2011). *10 Mindful Minutes.* Penguin Group, USA.

Luciani, J. (2007). *Self-Coaching.* Wiley and Sons Inc., USA.

Maxwell, J. (2007). *The Maxwell Daily Reader* . Yates and Yates Publishing, Nashville Tennessee, USA.

MacKenzie, T. (2016). *Dive Into Inquiry: Amplify Learning and Empower Student Voice.* Ed Tech Team Press. USA.

Meldrum, Kim. (2016). *Assessment That Matters: Using Technology to Personalize Learning.* Ed Tech Team Press. USA.

Olivia, M. (2009). *Beatitudes for the Workplace* . Novalis Press, Canada.

Palmer, P. (1990). *The Active Life: A Spirituality of Work, Creativity and Caring.* Harper Collins, New York, USA.

Palmer, P (1998). *The Courage to Teach.* San Fracisco: Jossey-Bass Inc., Publishers.

Pink, D. (2011). *DRIVE: The Surprising Truth About What Motivates Us.* Riverhead Books, New York., USA.

Reeves, D. (2009). *Leading Change in Your School.* ASCD Data, USA.

Ritchhart, R. (2015). *Creating Cultures of Thinking: The 8 Forces We Must Master to Truly Transform Our Schools.* Jossey-Bass, CA., USA.

Sharma, R. (2010). *The Leader Who Had No Title: A Modern Fable on Real Success and in Life.* Free Press. New York., USA.

Theoharis, G. & Brooks, J. (2012). *What Every Principal Needs to Know to Create Equitable and Excellent Schools.* Teachers College Publ. New York., USA.

Wiederkehr, M. (2008). *Seven Sacred Pauses.* Sorin Books, Notre Dame, Indiana, USA.

Wilson, D. & Conyers, M. (2016). *Teaching Students to Drive their Brains.* Association of Supervision & Curriculum Development. ASCD. USA.